If the
Girl
Never
Learns

If the
Girl
Never
Learns

poems

Sue William Silverman

Brick Mantel Books
Bloomington, Indiana

Published by Brick Mantel Books, USA

Brick Mantel
BOOKS

www.BrickMantelBooks.com
info@BrickMantelBooks.com

An imprint of Pen & Publish, Inc.
Bloomington, Indiana
(314) 827-6567
www.PenandPublish.com

Print ISBN: 978-1-941799-64-2
eBook ISBN: 978-1-941799-65-9

Library of Congress Control Number: 2018954332

Printed on acid-free paper.

Cover Photo © Peter Adams, Sydney, Australia:
Author, Ocean City boardwalk, New Jersey, 1973

Back Cover Author Photo © Angie Chen

for

Marc J. Sheehan, with love, always

Vermont College of Fine Arts
(my literary home)

all women who resist

Also by Sue William Silverman

POETRY

Hieroglyphics in Neon

CREATIVE NONFICTION

Because I Remember Terror, Father, I Remember You
(winner of the Association of Writers and Writing Programs
Award Series)
Love Sick: One Woman's Journey through Sexual Addiction
The Pat Boone Fan Club: My Life as a White Anglo-Saxon Jew

CRAFT

Fearless Confessions: A Writer's Guide to Memoir

Contents

The Girl and the Man

If the Girl Never Learns to Cook or Sew

then the scent of chlorine seeps beneath the glass
doors into winter.
If dinners simmer
on the stove into summer, spring, fall. If
the stuffed cat remains
by the door across from
the ivory-tipped walking sticks.
If the extravagant
bric-a-brac Santas
push you back
out the door. If the family man's
promises, promises, promises
go up in the pungent smoke of *good-bye*. This girl,
who slouches on her chair, her single piece of real
estate, not allowed to touch couch or dining room table.
If waves break
like vows across the dunes,
foam at midnight, and as faithless.

If the words the girl sighs
aren't stitched intricately as patchwork
hanging on the line to dry. If this
girl/woman in mismatched
socks, hair refusing to shrink
into tight gray curls. . . .

If he says *no* and *yes*
on the same day, and you drive black
asphalt straight ahead while glancing in the rear-
view mirror. If he's so clever saying *yes* and *no*,
all that remains in your unspoken throat
is *maybe*. If he laughs and offers one of his canes,
you know damn well you're walking
alone and forever.
If the *yes*es and *no*s don't equal *maybe* but total *zero*.

If you're each heading in opposite
directions while stars float
away and sun shatters the sky.

If that's all you're getting, girl, then you're just this side
of running on empty not to know
this, but lost enough to understand *that*. If you turn
your head at just the right or wrong moment, but
definitely the wrong
angle and smudge red on his green-shirted heart. If
you worry it'll be misunderstood: don't. Because who can see
secret signs you breathe tracing his house?
If you knew the answer to the question, or the key to open
answers to questions not yet asked . . . but you don't.
Except you do.

If the Girl Never Tells the Man

A smudge of baby bleeds
into the toilet like red
crayons melting. Summer, the girl
in blue-and-pink tank top, cut-off
jeans, sweats onto linoleum, her thought-
less head raining ghosts in tutus. Brittle
flower petals crack. Memory
dissolves across night like fireworks
trailing sparks. The girl's silent
earth is scorched
with bones, her braids
unraveling their carefully
woven unknowing.

She never tells
the man
who whispers *her*
name, her name, her name
that she can't hear
in downed electrical
wires snapping damp
pavement. The girl wraps
her torso tight until her mind
forgets what her body doesn't:
the Rorschach sheet
outlining baby hands and feet.
She bakes oatmeal cookies
for afternoon tea sipped
from a chipped
cup while the cat exhales
leukemia. She offers him a crumb,
his fur mossy
with death,
which never comes and then it does.

If the Girl Becomes a Bridesmaid

Wedding guests come
and go, come
and go, heart-
shaped mercurial
candies sucked
between teeth
tight as hisses,
mechanical
arms and legs screwed
into rusty
sockets . . . the bride wearing
wooly afghan,
a skull
embroidered in her
stomach . . . the groom
cultivating
moths down
in the basement, wedding
vows muttered
like curses:
is what the girl hopes will happen.
He, ignoring her,
as if he watches a blank
TV screen,
one disconnected, at that . . .
as if her desirable
limbs are wrapped
tight in a pastel
straitjacket.

If the Girl Fills out the Questionnaire

Always, the motel, one sheet
of paper. One pencil. One final
note. One
strand of hair looping
the scarred
desk carved with a pen knife. Names.
Phone numbers. Sex. Positions.
Not that it matters. Blanks
full of wrong answers or empty
questions circle disconnected phone
lines, ringing. The man's either home
or misplaced—but too scared
now
to answer.

If the Girl Stalks the Man

and rings his doorbell
that echoes through
a house untamable
as weather.

If he grabs her arm sleeved
in recklessness, the ticking
clock stops
at the worst possible
minute in the past.

His gaze is blank
as crockery, so the girl
conjures hairline
fissures, her desire bright

and wild as pollen.

If the Girl Thinks *Love Is Here Every Day!*

The girl darkens under the Jersey shore
boardwalk, black leather, hair
braiding her to the pillar,
where this promise is sprayed.

The Ferris wheel circles
the moon, the boardwalk
circles the earth.
A camera captures

her defiant acquiescence.
She reads a novel
about how her mouth
is pink cotton candy.

A man's tissue-
paper-thin breath trembles
in expensive moonlight.
His shirt, luminous

as wind, swirls a starlit
sky, she swallowing
a mouthful of it.
Tail-finned

cars speed toward Atlantic
foam. Salt bruises
her tongue. The season
is over. The girl's

smile is a last carousel ride,
wood horses distorted
in mirrors. She'd translate
her body back into its own
language, if only she could.

If the Girl Knows Where to Fuck

Up, down, sideways along a map's
red highways in stilettos

sharp as a cactus
crossing deserts,

in snow drifts
all through steppes,

pinned beneath stalactites
in musky caves,

inside hydrangeas, feverish
in hospital beds and crowded

in downtown morgues,
behind velvet pews

and incensed
altars, swirling

in sandstorms
of sweat, along subway

tunnels, woven
in spider webs, snuffed

inside smoke stacks,
and developing in voluptuous

photographs, zooming around
the equator of night.

Adrift on lily pads, slick
inside oysters, shooting up

in rockets. On conveyer belts
like an amusement park

ride that attracts
the desperate-to-feel-

alive. Inside clocks,
mesmerized by time

ticking backward. Behind
bars and *in* bars, pounding

on dance floors, in iron-pipe
motel rooms, out of control

in intersections
just as lights

change from green to caution
to stop.

If the Girl Sees New Horizons

I'm not the answer, says the man
unreachable as dry land.
But you're the question, the girl thinks.

The girl
rows on fully
believing in the vastness
of desire, of ache, of need,
into which she could
tumble eternally
and call it a day.

Seraphic gulls swarm
inside her skull.

The irises of her eyes
shimmer like oil floating
on the ocean all
the way to where it
meets the sky, seeing now
she has
to begin again, no matter how
much her mouth
is full of silence and salt.

If the Girl Wears the Man's Green Shirt

The orderly confiscates glass
vials of face lotion, nail
polish, the girl wanting to look
her best when she swirls down
the drain, stockpiling
meds in the pocket of the man's
shirt she stole

for company. Hammered
turtles smashed to green
clay smithereens before dinner
where they watch
her every move as if a plastic
knife could cause the mayhem
she's after. Lights
out. The girl naked

in the windowed sky, eyelashes studded
with stars blinding her
in the buzz of air
conditioning her to act
like a girl who doesn't steal
or stab or slit or fuck. They want her

to forget but she remembers
the way the men came one
after one after
one pounding motel
doors, waves churning
at her ankles, her knees,
her neck. Flat

on her back she evaporates in salty
perfunctory kisses
spinning her brain
until she staggers at the feet of

the man, the man, the man
who wraps her in kudzu—

dense and thick.
Invasive.

If the Girl Considers Revenge

Daily, monthly,
yearly, fever minute
by minute spiking incre-
mentally from the girl's
house to the man's
burning images of a wife
standing blind guard
on her husband's
heart. Nausea rises.
The girl's fingernails—
yellow with rage—ragged
with grief . . . her pulse
erratic, flattening
her spine thin
as hope against
the mattress waiting
for nuclear winter or dengue or
vampire bats tracking
a sky already black as
funereal lace.
Who knows? She
might live forever. Only
her anger
will last longer.

If the Girl Could Learn a Skill

The girl waves good-
bye to the man
where he stands on the bow
of a ship, his wind-
breaker gusting
resilient red nylon, his arm
around his wife's
Hawaiian pink. They
both say *appease*
for the camera, but only
he sees the girl
in the fisheye lens.

I feel devoted
to her . . .
loyalty rising
like a moon's
sickle—a scythe
carving futures
like cardboard
cutouts on a deserted
movie set.

The last fumes
of night, scented black-
berries stain
stars, blinking
off one by one.

She spears fish
for a living,
and so pierces
his jaw with a hook,
gaffing him to
the deck, slicing
him open, revealing
his tasteful
and poisonous emptiness.

If the Girl Becomes an Assassin

The man and his wife walk the *Ponte dei Sospiri*,
holding hands, the man's forehead
in the crosshairs, the girl's finger
on the trigger.

Does she dare?

Would this result in parole,
oblivion, or being sentenced to seeing
behind the man's Venetian mask,
his blue eyes, for twenty years,
or, with good behavior, life?

How crazy can she go with two IVs
of Valium dripping between
knuckles? The girl asks the doc
if she can pop
Klonopin if she awakens
in the middle of her sentence.
Only if you want to wake up blue.

I do. I do.

Venice canals burn azure,
Nocturne in Blue and Gold, the hunchbacked
boatman rows the girl past severed heads
bobbing in currents that flow
from heaven to the sea—smoky

ether gusting from train engines,
Anna K.'s body segmenting
into thousands of sequels . . .
Emma B.'s mouth forming a perfect *O*,
all the women, heads in ovens,
the roots of their hair turning ashen
from lack of oxygen or love.

Her finger squeezes
the burnished
trigger almost hard
enough.

If the Girl Doesn't Become an Assassin

The bones in the girl's ankles crumble
like ancient bricks, her head pressed
against a black window, screaming
bloody blue murder
silently waiting for the release, for
her forehead to shatter, her soul
in exile behind high-voltage wire,
burn marks on her palms—
a mark, a tattoo, a brand

for the insane who wander
among unsuspecting shoppers,
the girl perfectly incapable
of putting a new strait-
jacket on layaway,
also gas masks, hazmat suits,
first-aid kits, last-rites' paraphernalia,
and bomb shelters strong
enough to withstand the critical
mass of her hydrogen
heart exploding.

The Girl and the Myth

If the Girl Is Reborn as a Mummy

descending the staircase,
her winding cloth
pooling onto the floor
like a player-piano scroll
of ancient blues.

A rainbow the color
of snakes,
forked tongues masquerading
as sparrow wings at dusk.

The plagues are
leprosy, cholera,
tuberculosis, lice, rickets,
and love—the latter
masked, a disease
otherwise shapeless, seeping
through stone blocks to the
desert beneath.

Even in
this life, or un-life, or
anti-life, the man translates
her hieroglyph for
Love as *Devastation*, the kind
that lasts.

If the Girl Enforces Overdue Fines

Night shift, behind
the checkout
counter, the girl balances
one penny
atop another,
a ridiculous Sisyphean
hill, precarious
as stacks
of books that
customers, ghostly
in florescence,
return one
after another . . .
homeless sweatshirts bleeding
the dye of their lonely
logos as the bodies
inside them settle
down for the long
haul, or closing, whichever
shoos them out first.
A toothless man,
some secret DJ,
cold cigarette
in his shapeless
mouth, spins
disco records, *Xanadu*
settling like dust-
magic or asbestos.
His audience
is captive by
circumstance, chance,
or choice.

Still they come,
automatic
door swinging
open/shut
in/out
books, books, books
shelves of how
to survive cancer or
love or loss or fix
a Kawasaki motorcycle.
The girl has a Dewey
Decimal system
dream. In it,
every page of every
book is pristine
and therefore
able to be shelved
anywhere. The girl
refuses the patrons'
plea to translate
the blankness. She needs
the money.

If the Girl Knew Who She Was

She steps into darkness un-
afraid in a man's 1940s
fedora, flicks
a fingernail against
a tumbler of musty scotch
in motel rooms abandoned after
she slithers through the key
hole slippery and wet.

She'll pour gas
down your chimney, cowering
in full view, if she has to,
holding out to you
damp matches.

Her love is
purple and black,
but only before
she bathes in bleach.

As it is,
she's a warning, a sign, an error,
a mummy sworn to silence,
a birthmark whose disputed, opaque borders
define who she isn't,
but not who she is.

If the Girl Is the Sorcerer's Apprentice

On a make-
shift stage,
a mirror ball sparkling him,
the magician saws the girl
in half. He announces
he'll kiss her body back
together, but every kiss
cuts the girl
until she's drained
of color, de-
composing, wild
narcissus keeping
her two halves
apart.

If the Girl Ungoes to War

Pirates unfuck her cunt,
unplucked from sockets,
eyes unfixed, undilated,
can't unwitness every unkind
crime, every unjoy.

Seas unlush
with bloody
unrooted hair swarm
with unkempt men,
the ends of whose arms still
handed, as yet unhooked,
are still ungentle.

The girl waves
a black flag, unsurrendering
her remains to
the unfuture of museums
depicting the unlost art of
revenge.

If the Girl Escapes a Bosch Painting

after Saint Wilgefortis (Santa Librada)

Miraculous hair beards
Librada's face, virgin-
ity intact, palms raped
to the cross, red-
dripped Portuguese
dress, a silver
slipper slides
from her foot, plucked
by a pilgrim fiddler
as if he could un-
strum her, her hymn
to god non-
binary, her saintly
death awaiting a skeletal
scythe to un-
hinge her father,
her harsh beard strangling
her cruel suitor's
neck. Mystical, myth-
ical screams awake
the mini-skirt
girl, an avatar
piercing men
with cathode-ray
vision, lenses in gold-
rimmed glasses burning
the lust in their
corneas, a wicked
smile hiding
kisses before
they grieve.

If the Girl Refuses

Lost in the city, the girl stumbles past abandoned boats knocking against docks. She's somewhere in the terra incognita of drunk, scotch crashing in her ears, rushing barefoot, discovering continents of loose nails, the man, smelling of rust, following her past warehouses bereft, even, of emptiness.

The man strips her bare, pushes her back against splinters, ties her up in the mephitic hull of a ship littered with dying synaptic signals, snapped off from cells. He plows through the girl's skin, muscle, and bone, tosses her in.

At the bottom of the ocean a glued-together horse, derelict with driftwood, nudges her spine. The horse plods through undersea currents, the girl passive on his back, breathing only through contact with his hide. The horse trudges onward until he deposits the girl at the edge of her body, miles above the equator, by the shore of some other, impossibly tranquil sea.

If the Girl Turns the World Upside Down

walking on her hands
exploring Blackbeard's Castle,
one palm in front
of the other—
hair dusting
fever grass and the cracked
limestone floor—
Madras shorts sliding
down/up her thighs, seductive,
because did he, or she, really
sink beneath
the waves?

Later, the girl cruises
Route 17 in her doubloon-
colored, Rangoon-red-leathered
Plymouth, past disaffected
Jersey boys loitering corners,
a bottle of underage
scotch between her legs.
Driving straight but drunk and
in reverse, for all
she knows, dashboard lit,
circling asphalt
like it's a black scarf,
a sun-warmed boa,
constricting its grip.

She has no place to sleep,
so she won't, preoccupied
as she is, with seaworms, salt
air, cannon smoke, warped
masts, frayed
sails—just another night
in the break-down

lane of mangled
axles, tire rims,
wheel covers, discarded
St. Christopher medals,
and bottle-tops——souvenirs
of mishaps, accidents,
and Acts of God
knows what.
She has
the only map to this
hoard of pirate loot.
No, that's wrong. She is
the map.

If the Girl Is a Sibyl above the Last Exit on the New Jersey Turnpike

Dusk, guardian bats cling—angelic,
beatific—to the girl's ribs. She
levitates above the overpass
awaiting her dead lover,
a man she would have
stabbed or shot
if he hadn't committed
suicide-by-alcohol as if it were
a piece of performance art lacking
only an encore.

The girl's rib
cage shudders, her spine
unzips, cracking open.
The bats circle her exhaust-
coiled hair like a purple
fleshy halo, fluttering feverish
desire scented with perfumed
blood—tempting
him to return from his hiding
place in the black wings.

The dead lover appears via
a Ouija board dressed not
for a séance but a soiree
in an unbuttoned shirt
revealing his shamelessness.
He offers the girl neon
dildos and the same old
excuses—slugs for the
toll booth bucket
and a map with *X*s
carefully marking
all the places
there will never be any treasure.

If the Girl Wears an Artificial Eye

It's like X-ray
glasses advertised
on the backs of comic
books, only a quarter,
to see straight through
clothes, skin, bones
into the soul—
transparent as river
ice—splintering
under the weight
of a boot,
or when the ruin
of love decays
one tooth after the other
until your head slips
off its neck, tumbling
into the past, before
you are born, when the soul
resembles blank
film upon which
any image you choose
might one day appear
as if developing, blooming
in darkroom chemicals.
The girl's glassy
eye might see
you as random
subterranean
trains clacking
into uncertain
futures, or violet
spines of ancient
texts imbued with answers
explaining loss

in Latin, Hebrew, or Greek, revealing
secrets secreted
in a Victorian house,
or else strobing light
atop a pyramid
flashing emergencies
across desert
sand and stars, or a slurry
of inky coal blasting
homicides down
a mountainside.
The soul leaks
into the drain
of a discarded
bathtub rimmed
with rust and regret.
But if she plucks
out her artificial
eye and inserts
the real deal
images vaporize
into smoke, mist,
fog, dust—the residue
of a puddle of rainwater—
and she'll see nothing,
nothing at all.

If the Girl Is a Horror Movie Starlet

Scene 1

Slice by slice, curls of rosewood peel
away. The girl poses on the floor,
nude, the father re-creating his daughter.
She'll never leave him, this wood girl.
He holds a chisel, she,
palms empty, arms modestly
crossed against the cold. Her legs
bent, for once, pressed
together, the girl, the father, watching
the sculpture form shoulders
and elbows, a rose vein in the wood
emerging from the neck, trailing
between breasts and thighs
as if filled with blood.

Scene 2

Mutant daddy longlegs slide
down the roof of the girl's green
Volkswagen bug, the car only in second
gear, crawling, the girl still miles
away from the crash. His thinner-
than-a-pin legs track the windshield,
the girl afraid to crank open the window.
She switches on wipers—dismembered
legs, his smashed body, smear
the glass. The wipers continue
to scrape back and forth,
until the credits roll.

Scene 3

Now the father
sits strapped in a lounge
chair. Otherwise, his waning
brain would scheme him away: his genius.
The girl sits beside him dipping a spoon
into a bowl of frozen, sweetened cream.
She slides it into his mouth.
He swallows greedily, nods
his head, unable to speak,
demanding more.

If the Girl Sprouts Wild Orchids from Her Hair

1.

The wife rocks
in her chair
breaking the girl's fingers under
runners, the sound of ice cracking,
the girl unable
to caress the man
who doesn't belong
to her anyway.

2.

The stallion's white mane rises
and falls past the girl's
window, her hair
wild with tropical
sleep, the floor beneath
her bare feet pounding
to the beat
of the stallion's
hooves or perhaps
her heart.

3.

The night newspaper obits
the man's death
and she imagines the rose
birthmark that flamed
his chest fading,
ashen by the time
the black truck
pulls into position.

4.

At the grave-
yard the girl is pushed
into the pit, women
yanking out her hair,
a ruler by which she is measured
by others, who cook and sew,
whose dream-orchids
wither in their sleep.

5.

If only she'd leapt
from the window
when she had the chance,
her body stretched
across the stallion's.
If only she'd gripped
his mane until she
outdistanced that life.

If the Girl Prepares to Feed a Cannibal in a Dark Alley

The girl crams her pockets
with bullets, one grenade, two
cubes of sugar. She sticks needles
under her fingernails. She eats
razors for breakfast, disjoints
her shoulders for lunch, but can't
decide what to kill for dinner.

Fog from the Gulf loosens
bricks, whole walls crumbling
toward her body, her bare
soles stumbling through spent
condoms, bells from dead
cats, beaks of ravaged birds,
reflections from windows,
silhouetted shades
casting neon tints of distorted
desire . . . she follows the scent
of his shadow . . . the way

she sniffed glue in nursery, licked
crayons in first grade, and wore
her dress and under-
pants inside out. She chewed every
other page of superhero comic
books: half as strong as Wonder
Woman, is strong enough.

But the girl could take
his hand and show him
love, whisper in his blue
eyes as she feeds him
the sugar, raw. The girl's heart
is *this* big, bigger than
this, deeper than

that . . . it is a ferocious delicacy,
one she must
resist giving to him,
despite the fact she has,
she thinks, no other
use for it.

If the Girl Loses Her Soul

Tattered sheets slink in shadows, hide
behind galvanized shutters, shrouding
the scent of red brick alleyways of
insert city name here, or the dark
side of heaven . . . does it matter?
Or maybe the girl plummets
from *here* to *anywhere*, her neon
hair blazing.

The girl, bloody as gauze,
her mouth sealed
shut, dirty kisses smeared
across her face, on her finger
a wedding ring the color
of verdigris at dusk, tarnished
windows reflecting a face draped
in frayed lace.

The girl's soul slips out
to search no-parking
zones for pennies, the ante
she needs for playing
afternoon tea, five-card stud,
or the cheapest jukebox
this side of a husband sleeping
so soundly she could place
this change on his eyes
and call it a life.

If the Girl Swallows Her Rosary

In a spring field the girl, hair
adorned with a garland
of Glorious roses, seeks

penance by stuffing black-
berries, round as beads,
into her mouth, her last

resort, Sorrowful
Mysteries like black
liquid seeping Luminous

veins, confessing
to the surgeon, she, seeking
Cures and Forgiveness,

he, slicing skin, the most intimate
moment of her life, a man
dissecting muscles, capillaries,

cells, organs no one before
has Witnessed, a scalpel
releasing psalms and heart-

beats—still as a Meditation—
quiet as a fossilized pulse—
a catacomb of arid

Desire trapped inside
marrow doused by sulphur,
formaldehyde, the girl exhaling

Sacraments, Praise lost
to memory, a faint apparition
flickering, ascending like an eternal

flame, palms burning an inky
sky, a fugitive from the City
of Grace.

If the Girl Never Writes on the Tower of Babel

The sky presses down too hard
to breathe, the girl exhaling
a million empty

cookies, no slips
of paper promising never
to come true, but that's

another country. After
the dance at the Jewish
Community Center, the girl

ignores the back window's
foggy '68 Chevy hieroglyphs—
his fingers probing

elastic for her secret
opening, but whispering the wrong
offerings . . . the girl weeping all

along the rivers of Babylon—
sorrowful, wordless, ancient.
When she hears from him never

again it is confusing,
confounding as the Torah,
his silence timeless.

Latin declensions spill out of her
mouth upside down. She forgets
how to spell *loss* in 6,900

languages. She fucks men in foreign
accents that sound exactly
the same. When she erases

the blackboard all
that remains are ghostly
equations too faint to translate.

If the Girl Considers Salvation

1.

The girl slides a white linen
tablecloth beneath the smear
of a deer in the break-
down lane, candelabra, candles
flickering, beside a billboard
of Jesus Christ on
the cross rapturous
in a field of frozen corn.

2.

The hospice in the middle
of a forest, one ghost per bed,
silent TV and radio, floor spit
polished reflecting wisps
of departing souls seeping
beneath pine planks,
through locked windows.

3.

Do you know who Jesus is?
the sign asks, and asks.
No. But this makes not knowing
who *she* is seem
that much more mysterious.

If the Girl Walks into Lake Michigan

Nightly, the girl snaps her arms onto her shoulders, her legs onto her hips, each finger and toe into the correct socket, matching knuckles. She maneuvers her heart into her chest, carefully attaching veins and arteries to prevent leakage. Her kneecaps creak, but are soothed by foamy waves.

She searches the littoral berm in moonlight for the havier, his celibate heart, his lowered head. He is the girl's perfect love: animal, chaste. She lies beside him, her forehead on his chest, his breath slowing.

One night she follows his tracks past the last sand bar, where they disappear. The girl with unhinged parts would eagerly loan him a leg, a foot, an eye—but so much is missing. How does she go on?

If the Girl Considers Predestination

1.

IV drips. Brain
fever floats on an ice floe,
Mercury in retrograde, memory
chips predicting
the end of her future.

2.

Ghost babies cling
to the hem
of her velveteen dress.
The girl, disguised
as a serving knife, carves.

3.

In the distance
a plane tumbles
from a cloud,
its black box hoarding
unavoidable mistakes.

The Girl and the End

If the Girl Does Phone Sex

Show me your bathroom faucet,
I'll show you my ripe pomegranate . . .
I want to swallow your rice pudding and have
you lick my pumpkin hollow.
Bored, the girl files
fingernails painted the color
of commercial lust.
Man after man,
all night long, her brain spins
a different script
from pouty lips. She doubts
any of her callers know the difference
between their cock and the snout
of an aardvark.

I want to hang myself, he says,
3 a.m., the girl
about to say she's no
Suicide Hotline, but offers
instead a scenario involving
Fruit Loops, her cunt,
and a can of Silly String,
which is better, anyway,
than dangling from
a cellar beam like a side
of kosher pork. Maybe
she's finally gone too far, but
she hears him there on his
end of the line, breathing.
Hard.

If the Girl Is a Slut

The girl's fever rises like exploding
thermometers, mercury sizzling
her palm, dancing in lavender
chiffon, a slight gust
to the hem, swirling
in the man's arms.

Show me a good time, baby. And
she does. Ravenous zippers, stripping.
Clouds wafting on floors
lavish with weather, fucking
in season, railroad tracks splintering
bedroom floors, her teeth rattling
in the aftermath.

Never mind the gang
rape as an excuse, the pawned
heart happened in another decade,
Route 17, Jersey, where chemicals
grow grass unnaturally green,
clouds light the sky
like overripe neon
relentless as brightly
used needles.

What would her Russian ancestors say?
They who risked pogroms, starvation,
inhuman soldiers clashing red
and white, just so their waiting-
to-be born daughter could slit
her crotch all the way up
to her mouth.

The girl torches all the photos.
No one's looking, or left to know,
except the mutant, half-formed

baby slithering down
the drain one night
when only *you & you*
were watching—as if it, too,
were simply lost
to the diaspora, the girl
not even bothering to cry,

especially when Houston's flooding—
cars wash to sea in hurricanes bright
as tangerines. The girl opens
doors and windows inviting
all the men in as if it's the Fourth of July,
her lips ripe and independent,
plummy for kissing
him to death, and the girl
only wishes he'd come back
to life so she could kill him
again.

If the Girl Is a Country-Western Ballad

1.

The little girl hangs upside
down on the jungle-
gym, her under-
pants yellow, white lace.
Blood rushes down
to her scalp . . .
dust wafts
up, sprinkling her
eyebrows and tangled
hair. Once, she tumbled
off: a small gash
on her elbow, droplets
in sand, a bruise
on her chin that lasts.

2.

With a red-lacquered nail,
the girl dials numbers
on her black
rotary phone, hoping to find
him home, then
randomly asks
for anyone's husband,
inserting her voice
like it's a sultry
one-line song.

3.

A doctor with delicate
surgeon hands combs
her hair, re-stitches the rip
on her elbow, shakes his head
over the bruise on her chin
that lasted all
this time, the doctor
treating her
chronic emergency.

4.

Shiner beer and drunk
thighs . . . dancing
the two-step at the Moulin Rouge
in Galveston, sawdust
floor, bare
legs and arms,
someone, anyone
pressing his hips
hard against hers,
skirt wafting up
as he pulls
her under-
pants down—
and they do it right
there . . . because this
is her song, one
no one puts
a quarter in the juke-
box to hear.

If the Girl Goes to the Next Whisky Bar

after Jim Morrison

She grooves to the back
beat of the Lizard King's cravings,
choking on scotch-soaked
cubes, suspending lust from
bar to blue narcotic lounges,
electrical surges, sex
with a disembodied
heart on a floor of smashed
cups and gypsy tea leaves
mute and unforseeing.
The next bar, the next
reptilian tongue, kiss tasting
of flayed leather—
desire rolling holy
with never enough to
drink/breathe/swallow/fuck,
his signature Mojo
moan risin',
from a bathtub combustible
with desperation—
legions of French
foreignness piquing
his last dull interest
in Parisian cathedral bells
that *clank, conk, gong, bong, peal*,
and *ring ring ring* signaling
time to move on to the next
happiest hour
after you are
gone, the girl
spilling Walker on
the floor of the bar as if
over your grave, drinking
whatever's left in her glass.

If the Girl Unzips Her Body

Willow leaves, popcorn, Jujubes, a polka-
dotted knuckle bone, silk ribbons corseting
ribs memorable as a xylophone. Plastic rainbows
overarch the wattage
of Vegas. Bits of a prescription
dissolve on her tongue . . . a catalogue
advertising expensive remedies flashing
red and blue
be-bop, hip-hop, and *rock.*

A papier-mâché wedding
certificate. A divorce
decree written in licorice. Rice
powder and lace, sapphires
and rubies, bits of gravel. An attic
of Christmas tinsel insulating
rubber bands, twine, a miniature
cyst, and a stuffed blue dog,
stitching ripped, waiting
for a walk.

A black-and-white photo
of the girl with a gray sunflower
woven in her braid. A gardenia
corsage with brown edges. Bell-
bottom jeans and gypsy blouses.

Arteries crisscross out-of-date
maps. A diaphragm exhales dreams
of flying fish and nightmares
of a salt-water mouth.
Ghostly carbon
paper of lost words
imprint a heart otherwise
undisturbed, otherwise

why would she let it
beat
right where anyone could erase it?

If the Girl Has Irrepressible Memories

The girl stands on the skin
of the earth, the moon so close
she waves to children wearing jumpers
and jeans. On the next turn
she grabs the Sea of Tranquility like a carousel's
brass ring.

A field sprouts people
leafy as soybeans.
From one of the rows a man plants
his fist between her legs, requiring
the girl to explain the way
babies can be born without
eyes or hands or heat.
The girl, diurnal,

cycles another year, seeding
a field of inedible vegetables,
thistles, and thirst.
The nocturnal girl looks

for the man. But all the pages
of her borrowed books shed
glue and cracked
bindings, becoming a badly
translated constellation
of extinct stars.

The man clasps the girl's
honeysuckle hair while she drizzles
more seeds in her roots:
lavender, citrus, rose.

The man blossoms into
unmagical beans—the girl
plants them,
scythe in hand. Ready.

If the Girl Never Learns What She Learned

The *sleep, sleep, sleep*
of formaldehyde, the scent
of yellow sapphires, the color of
diamonds, emeralds, rubies.
For you, girl, there's no hope.

From pink to blue her fingernails rise
one by one by one. The music
needles her scalp, thoughts leak
soft as mud. The girl's hair
is scorched as a turtle shell
crisp in the sun's unrelenting bake.

Gulls explode into brainless
feathers littering the shore.
This is everything she doesn't
know. Everything she does
will take longer to accept.

If the Girl Receives a Caress from a Man without Hands

The girl's forehead steams,
her feet wandering Jerusalem's old city, passing
stalls of silver, turquoise, carnelian,
embroidered dresses, the shop-
keeper slipping billowy green
over her head, his stubby
wrists, wounds tight as grenades,
grazing her shoulders . . . *yet gentle*,
she thinks, *no thorny nails*
or bony knuckles. She places coins
on an enamel plate without
expecting change.

In air scented by olive trees,
the girl dreams of hands severed
by bayonets—the man entering
her chamber dripping blood—
a kind of tenderness
like cancer curling up
snug inside bones, radiated skin
rainbowed pink, lavender, gold—fragile
as parchment—a surgical dig—
an archaeologist discovering
every damaged
cell in her body.

The girl returns to the shopkeeper's
stall to grasp his handless
hands, his stubs,
as if she can mend
him, or as if he could press
his phantom palm
between her legs
and call it love.

If the Girl Is Slow to Love

The mute swan glides
shadows, parting
pollen, the girl's
gaudy desire—
the man behind
her pressing palms
to her white neck,
the girl's love

asleep at the bottom
of a blind lake—bubbles
rupturing arteries—
a moon heavy
as loss slowing
the earth until it's
a still life, a silent
film's final
The End.

If the Girl Envisions Death

Where does the throb in your heart go
when it stops? Who will care for it?

Where do veins go
when blood foams under your fingernails?
Where does the flutter of lungs go
when they slow to a shudder? It slips
out reverberating in dark streets, useless.

The crease between
your eyebrows splits your skull,
breath slips
past your lips.

The sun is fragile.
The moon flickers when
the breeze disappears.
Your pupils don't
know what to see so they see
everything and nothing.

You are a hint of air seeping through glass.
Your palm presses against
a flash of light.

Moisture curdles.
Your shadow is twice
as large as your outline.
Your name is engulfed in
blue. It slides toward you
but is too exhausted to sing.

If the Girl Says the End Is Near

The girl crochets maimed
hearts resulting in ill-
shaped snocksnarles,
then stands over
a stove boiling
them with all the damaged
souls she's racked up . . .

the stew foaming,
spilling over
the sides of a dented
aluminum pot, brewing
miniature versions
of men and women
the girl once trampled
or gored—bubbling,
curdling, in one
giant, Boschian
clusterfuck.

A black camper van delivers
the girl to the first
right past Saturn, or
the last exit off
a saffron desert, or
to tunnels below
subways where
the girl's last token
affords her a death
of choice.

If the girl never learns
will her neck bend
under a tumorous weight?
Will misguided cells slit
her arteries and byways
from her tongue
to her toes?

If the girl had it all
to do over, she'd choose
the same mistakes or ones
even grander—emptying her womb
of death until everyone sees,
as if behind frosted glass,
every sin, every loss,
every sorrow.

If the Girl Goes to Hell in an Overnight Bag

The girl packs her pink alligator
bag decorated with cavitied teeth
and decaying posies, full with a poodle

skirt, a map of New Jersey,
sunscreen, Aqua Net hair spray,
sarcophagal eyeliner—and plunges

down toll-free tunnels
of coal, diamonds, skeletons,
rabbits fucking like rabbits.

Boys and girls, dead
anyway, snuff
film extras, snap selfies.

Tanning in her polka-dot
bikini, her skin ravaged
yellow, indolent, glassy,

the girl sighs, her pulse
steady as death.
Mutters and whispers,

lawless streets, an off-key
drum heralding
each arrival at the motel

advertising neon razor blades,
remorse under glass,
and complimentary

despair—everything
she'd hoped for—and more.
She wears a dress sewn

from skin
and licks blood
from between the seams—

her own eternal evening gown.
She stumbles into a dizzy
dream vacation

home for her soul.
Despite having paid
in advance, the girl

has no reservation—
has no reservations
at all.

If the Girl Dies, or Doesn't

The girl awakens in a pink-satin-lined coffin,
unlaced combat boots, a corsage
of chiffon lace cascading to ankles, blood
from a carotid artery sponged
neat and dry. Didn't cut
deep enough. Imitation
strychnine only slowed her heart.

Haunting Kiev seeking
strychnine scammers,
combat boots trudging
snowy drifts, Ukrainian troops,
pro-Russian rebels, 3,700 bodies stiff
as steppes. The girl tramps grave-
yards of her own long-dead
ancestors—blinded by bitter wind—
or seeing skeletons
embracing their forevers.

There's a border between
life and death and she's
crossed it, or perhaps erased it.
Her passport has a thumbnail
photo like an obituary
headshot. If a guard challenges her
to show her papers,
she'll say she's an expatriate
from life and dare him
to send her back.

Acknowledgments

With deep gratitude to Jennifer Geist and Brick Mantel Books.

Many thanks to the following journals for publishing individual poems. Some of these poems have been published under different titles and in different versions.

Bellingham Review
> "If the Girl Never Learns to Cook or Sew"
> "If the Girl Is a Sibyl above the Last Exit on the New Jersey Turnpike"
> "If the Girl Receives a Caress from a Man without Hands"
> "If the Girl Knows Where to Fuck"

Blackbird
> "If the Girl Refuses"

Blue Lyra Review
> "If the Girl Turns the World Upside Down"

Cultural Weekly
> "If the Girl Stalks the Man"
> "If the Girl Thinks *Love is Here Every Day!*"

december
> "If the Girl Is a Country-Western Ballad"

Diode Poetry Journal
> "If the Girl Wears the Man's Green Shirt"
> "If the Girl Prepares to Feed a Cannibal in a Dark Alley"

Drunken Boat
> "If the Girl Sprouts Wild Orchids from Her Hair"

Dunes Review
> "If the Girl Walks into Lake Michigan"

Hotel Amerika
"If the Girl Knew Who She Was"
"If the Girl Loses Her Soul"
"If the Girl Never Writes on the Tower of Babel"
"If the Girl Considers Salvation"

Independent Noise
"If the Girl Sees New Horizons"

Nasty Women Poets: An Unapologetic Anthology of Subversive Verse,
Lost Horse Press
"If the Girl Considers Revenge"

Ninth Letter
"If the Girl Does Phone Sex"

Painted Bride Quarterly
"If the Girl Ungoes to War"

Red Sky: Poetry on the Global Epidemic of Violence Against Women,
Sable Books
"If the Girl Is a Horror Movie Starlet"

Zone 3
"If the Girl Is the Sorcerer's Apprentice"
"If the Girl Wears an Artificial Eye"

CPSIA information can be obtained
at www.ICGtesting.com
Printed in the USA
BVHW030804020419
544357BV00001B/20/P